THE ROMANS

FACT AND FICTION

Adventures in Roman Britain

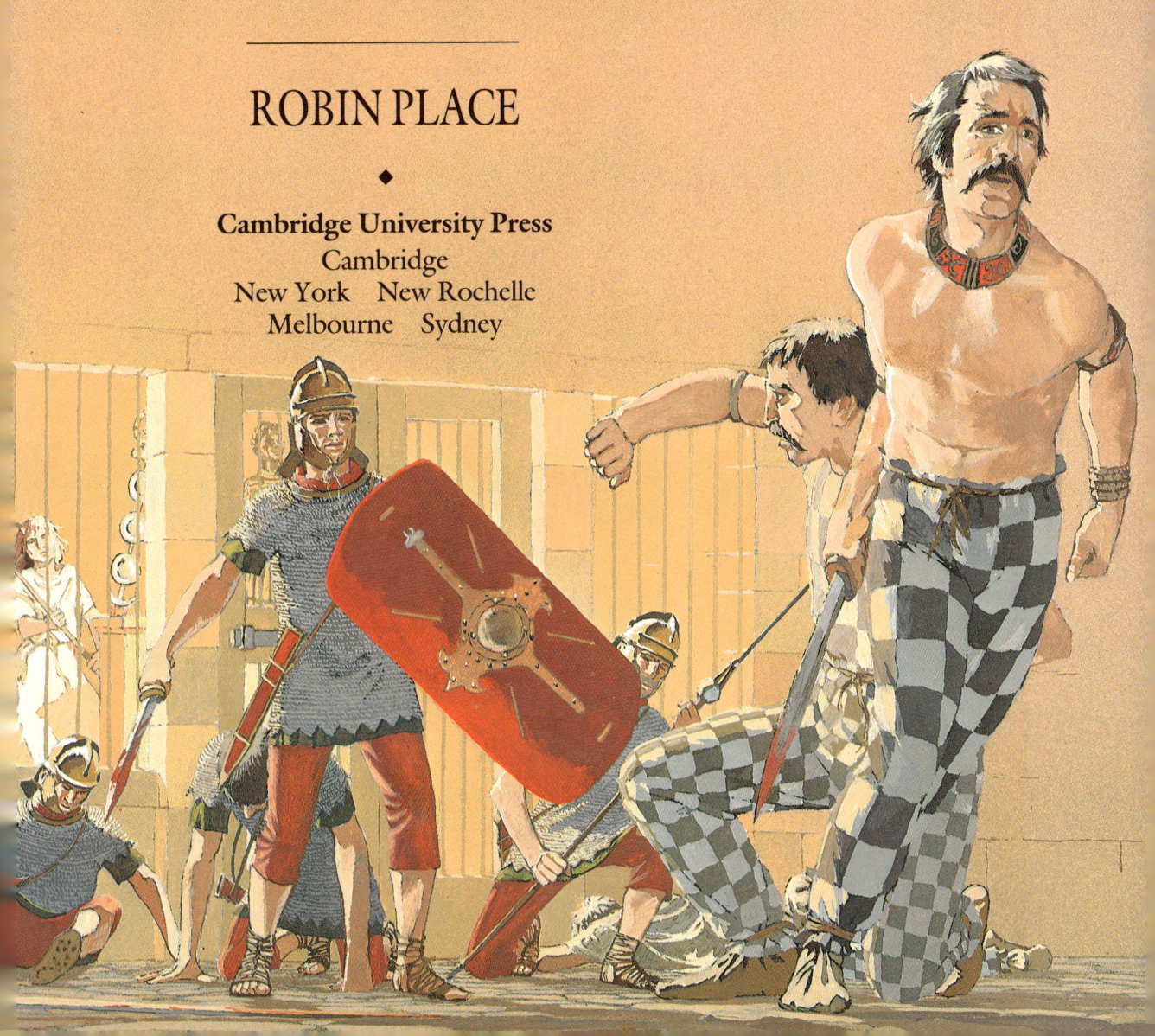

ROBIN PLACE

◆

Cambridge University Press
Cambridge
New York   New Rochelle
Melbourne   Sydney

Published by the Press Syndicate of the University of Cambridge
The Pitt Building, Trumpington Street, Cambridge CB2 1RP
32 East 57th Street, New York, NY 10022, USA
10 Stamford Road, Oakleigh, Melbourne 3166, Australia

© Cambridge University Press 1988

First published 1988

Printed in Great Britain by W. S. Cowell Ltd, Ipswich

British Library Cataloguing in publication data
Place, Robin
The Romans: fact and fiction: adventures in Roman Britain.
1. Romans – Great Britain – Juvenile literature 2. Great Britain –
Social life and customs – To 1066 – Juvenile literature
3. Great Britain – History – Roman period, 55 B.C.-449 A.D. –
Juvenile literature
I. Title   II. Ryley, Chris
936.1'04   DA145

Library of Congress Cataloging-in-Publication Data
Place, Robin.
   The Romans: fact and fiction.
   Summary: Describes daily life in Roman Britain based on
evidence from archeological findings and follows the adventures
of two fictional characters living in Britain in 158 A.D.
   1. Romans – Great Britain – Juvenile literature. 2. Great Britain
– Antiquities, Roman – Juvenile literature. [1. Romans – Great
Britain. 2. Great Britain – Antiquities, Roman. 3. Great Britain –
History – Roman period, 55 B.C. – 449 A.D.] I. Ryley, Chris, ill.
II. Title.
DA145.P63 1987   936.2'04   86-32648

ISBN 0 521 33267 2 hard covers
ISBN 0 521 33787 9 paperback

DS

Illustrations by Chris Ryley

Acknowledgements

p4 (top and bottom right), p6, p8, p10 (top and bottom right), p22 (centre) Museum of London;   p4 (bottom left), p18 (top left), p20 (top left), p30 (top right) Trustees of the British Museum;   p10 (left) The National Maritime Museum, London;   p12, p14, p16, p33, front cover Sussex Archaeological Society;   p18 (top right), p28 (bottom left) The Hadrian's Wall Museums;   p18 (bottom left) Fototeca Unione, at the American Academy in Rome;   p20 (right), p24 Institute of Archaeology, University of Oxford;   p20 (bottom left), p22 (top left and bottom right) Bath Archaeological Trust;   p22 (bottom left), p28 (top right) Vindolanda Trust and University of Newcastle upon Tyne;   p26 (top left) the author;   p26 (top right) Mrs G. Rocke;   p26 (centre) Historic Buildings and Monuments Commission for England;   p26 (bottom left) Carlisle Museums and Art Gallery;   p26 (bottom right) University of Newcastle upon Tyne;   p28 (bottom right) Doncaster Museum and Art Gallery;   p30 (bottom right) Rheinisches Landesmuseum, Bonn.

Line drawings by Neil Sutton

What this book is about

These stories are about people who lived in Roman Britain. The places and the things in the stories are real, but the people are imaginary. At the time of the stories, AD 158, the Romans were the most powerful people in the world. Their huge Empire included England and Wales, which they called the Province of Britannia. It was ruled by two officials, the Governor, who commanded the army, and the Procurator, who collected taxes among other duties. The stories are about four places that you can visit:

- LONDINIUM (London) was a great port and the capital city. Archaeologists have found that it was becoming deserted by AD 158. They don't know why.
- FISHBOURNE ROMAN PALACE (we don't know its Roman name). A grand palace was built here in AD 75, but by AD 158, people lived only in the northern part, which was being rebuilt and new mosaic floors were being laid.
- AQUAE SULIS (Bath). Its Latin name means 'waters of the goddess Sulis'. It was a spa town, visited by tourists as it still is today.
- VERCOVICIUM (Housesteads) means 'the place of tough fighters'. It was an important fort on Hadrian's Wall. You can walk round the remains of the army buildings described in the last story.

The stories are about two families. Tiro and his family live in Londinium. He lays mosaics, helped unwillingly by his son Rufus, who would much rather be in the army. Tiro also has a daughter called Pacata. Valens is an official on the staff of the Procurator. He lives in Londinium with his wife and son Felix, who suffers from asthma. Felix is one of the lucky people who grow out of asthma at about 14, but Pacata thinks he is very strange until she gets to know him better. Felix' grandparents, Lucius and Mercatilla, live at Fishbourne and are converting the old palace into a new house.

When I was writing this book, I went to all the places I was writing about, looked at all the latest archaeological finds, and thought about what might have happened there. So that you can judge for yourself what the evidence is, we have shown places and finds on the 'How do we know?' fact pages opposite each story page.

I hope you will enjoy this journey back in time – by reading the stories, by looking at the evidence in this book and by going to see these Roman sites for yourself.

Robin Place

HOW DO WE KNOW?

The streets and houses of Londinium are 5–7 metres (16–23 ft) below the present City of London. Over the years, houses have been pulled down and new ones built over the ruins, so the ground-level has risen. Londinium has been rediscovered by workmen digging deep holes – for foundations, sewers, and the Underground. In the 17th century Sir Christopher Wren noted Roman remains when St. Paul's Cathedral was being built. Modern foundations have destroyed most of Londinium.

Archaeologists excavating a mosaic floor. It is like the ones Tiro laid and repaired. It is made of hundreds of little cubes of stone, called *tesserae*. ➤

This bronze head of the Emperor Hadrian was dredged from the River Thames in 1834. It could be part of the statue Pacata hid behind on the Roman bridge. ▼

There may be very little time between the demolition of an old building and the erection of a new one. Archaeologists often have to work while building is going on around them. ➤

Thank you, River God of Londinium

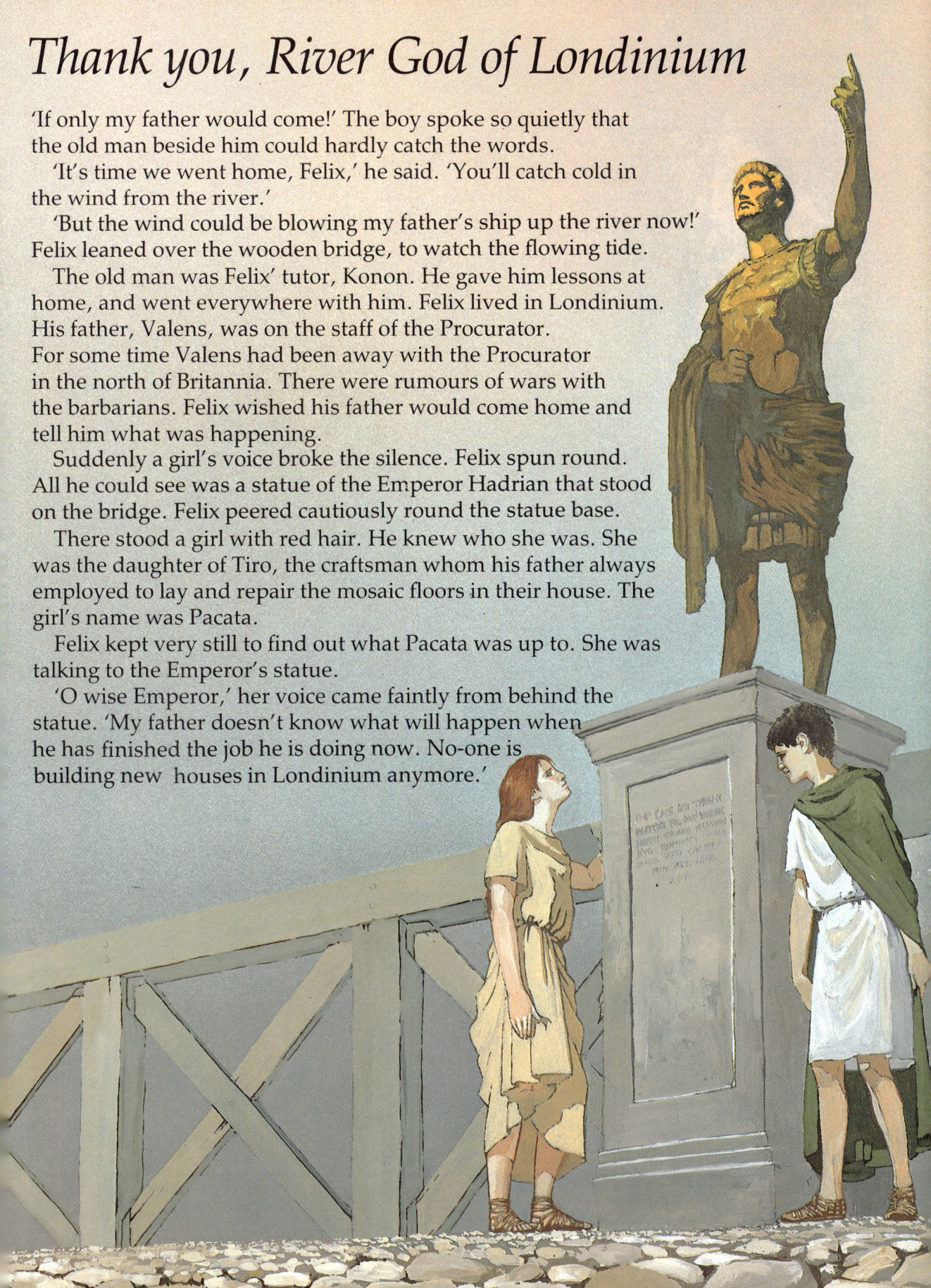

'If only my father would come!' The boy spoke so quietly that the old man beside him could hardly catch the words.

'It's time we went home, Felix,' he said. 'You'll catch cold in the wind from the river.'

'But the wind could be blowing my father's ship up the river now!' Felix leaned over the wooden bridge, to watch the flowing tide.

The old man was Felix' tutor, Konon. He gave him lessons at home, and went everywhere with him. Felix lived in Londinium. His father, Valens, was on the staff of the Procurator. For some time Valens had been away with the Procurator in the north of Britannia. There were rumours of wars with the barbarians. Felix wished his father would come home and tell him what was happening.

Suddenly a girl's voice broke the silence. Felix spun round. All he could see was a statue of the Emperor Hadrian that stood on the bridge. Felix peered cautiously round the statue base.

There stood a girl with red hair. He knew who she was. She was the daughter of Tiro, the craftsman whom his father always employed to lay and repair the mosaic floors in their house. The girl's name was Pacata.

Felix kept very still to find out what Pacata was up to. She was talking to the Emperor's statue.

'O wise Emperor,' her voice came faintly from behind the statue. 'My father doesn't know what will happen when he has finished the job he is doing now. No-one is building new houses in Londinium anymore.'

HOW DO WE KNOW?

In the 1970s, the warehouses of the London docks near London Bridge were pulled down. In the damp ground below them, archaeologists found huge oak timbers. These were the beams of the Roman waterfront, 80 metres (260 ft) inland from the present Thames. For many years, archaeologists have been trying to find the Roman bridge over the Thames. In 1981, a massive wooden structure 7 metres (23 ft) square and over 2.5 metres (8 ft) high was found. It was not part of the waterfront, but was built in the river itself. It was one of the piers of the Roman bridge.

← The bridge pier shown on a model of the bridge. It was built of oak timbers each 32cm (12.5 in) square.

An archaeologist measuring the timbers of the bridge pier. At the front of the photograph is a pump to keep the trench dry. →

All sorts of shoes were worn in Londinium, from light slippers to heavy hob-nailed boots. Women's shoes were made of brightly-coloured leather. None had high heels.

Here is a leather shoe with long laces. It is like the shoes Pacata threw into the river. ↑

↑ This is what the Roman Bridge would have looked like. It was about 5 metres (16 ft) wide. It stood just east of the present London Bridge.

A lace-up shoe with little holes cut out carefully all over it.
←

'If I give my shoes to the river god, do you think he will help my father to get more work? They're almost new, and the best thing I've got.'

The sun came out and shone on the Emperor's face. Was this a sign that he agreed? There was silence. Felix guessed that Pacata must be unwinding the long shoelaces from round her ankles. Then he saw her appear at the bridge rail. She held her shoes over the water for a moment. Then she let them drop.

Two pairs of eyes watched the shoes as they fell into the river with a splash. The shoes spun round on the surface for a moment, as if the river god was making up his mind whether or not to accept the gift. Then they sank.

Pacata looked round and saw Felix watching her. Her face turned as red as fire. Felix wanted to say that he hadn't meant to listen, but his breath wouldn't come. He often had attacks like this. He clung to the bridge wheezing, as Pacata ran off.

At last Felix could speak. 'Yes, I'll come home,' he gasped to his anxious tutor, 'but I want to go to a shop first.'

Pacata felt rather worried about going home. Her mother was going to be cross when she came home with bare feet, so she decided to go and meet her father outside the baths instead. He always went there after work to get clean and meet his friends. He would understand about her shoes.

But her mother was cross all the same. 'Where do you think the money's going to come from to buy a new pair?' she scolded. But by the time supper was over, she had got over it.

After supper, Pacata and her brother Rufus started a game of knucklebones on the floor. They took turns to throw five little bones from a sheep's foot in the air, and see how many they could catch on the back of one hand. Some evenings, Pacata would accuse Rufus of jogging her hand to make the bones fall off, so the game ended in a fight. But tonight, Pacata was on her best behaviour because of her shoes.

Their game was stopped by a knock at the door. Rufus got up to answer the door. He picked up a little clay lamp so that he could see his way from their living room at the back of the house through Tiro's workshop with its heaps of coloured stones.

Rufus came back laughing, holding something behind his back. 'That was one of Valens' slaves, with a gift to Pacata from Felix.' He handed Pacata the gift. It was a pair of shoes! 'However did he know you needed new shoes?'

But Pacata wasn't telling.

HOW DO WE KNOW?

The things that people lost or threw away are used by archaeologists to find out about everyday life in Londinium. The people of Londinium threw a lot of rubbish into the Walbrook, a river now running deep down in a big pipe, under the road called Walbrook near the Mansion House. Archaeologists have found many things made of wood and leather preserved in the wet ground there. In dry ground, only things made of stone and metal have survived.

← Part of a Roman basket from the Walbrook.

A bronze toilet set (enlarged). ▲These were worn hanging from a belt. There were tweezers to pluck out hairs (1), a scoop to clean wax from the ears (2), and a nail cleaner (3).

Roman craftsmen made lovely jewellery from gold and semi-precious stones. Bronze ornaments were cheaper.

Pacata's mother would have liked to buy a brooch like the one in this photograph. It is made of bronze and is in the shape of a bird with blue inlay on the wings. →

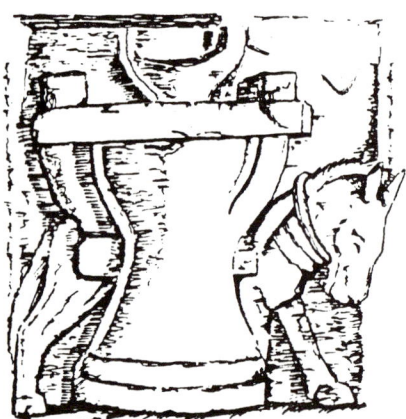

▲This stone carving shows a donkey turning a big millstone. A millstone like this was dug up in Princes Street, London, so there must have been a bakery there.

Next day, Pacata and her mother went shopping in the forum, the big market place. Markets were held every nine days. Pacata's school was closed then. The children were taught in a room in one of the buildings round the square market place. It had no door, only a curtain. On noisy market days, with stall-holders just outside shouting to people to buy their goods, the master would not have been able to hear the children recite their lessons.

On the way to market, Pacata's mother sighed as they passed rows of ruined buildings. 'When I was a child and went shopping with my mother, she told me that all these buildings used to be shops. In those days, ships were always arriving with jars of wine and lots of foreign food. It must have been lovely to be able to buy olives and fish-sauce.' Then there had been a terrible fire, in the reign of the Emperor Hadrian. No-one knew how it had started, but it had spread quickly among the wooden houses with their thatched roofs. Most of Londinium had been burnt down. After the fire, many people had moved to other towns, and merchants had not thought it worth setting up businesses in Londinium any more.

They soon came to the forum, where there were still lots of stalls. Pacata's mother liked stopping to look at necklaces and brooches, even though she didn't have any money to buy them. There were useful little toilet sets for sale, and cosmetics in glass bottles too. Pacata liked the smell of the perfume stall. Another lovely smell, of newly baked bread, came from the bakery. Pacata always went to the back of the shop to stroke the donkey that pulled the huge grindstone round that ground the corn into flour.

HOW DO WE KNOW?

A Roman ship was excavated at Blackfriars in 1962. It was a small sailing ship, flat-bottomed, 16 metres (52 ft) long and 6 metres (20 ft) wide. It carried a cargo of stone from Kent, and had sunk after a collision. Archaeologists know that it was a sea-going ship, because the timbers had been bored by worms that live only in salt water.

The Blackfriars ship would have looked like the boat on the right. It was steered with a large paddle at the stern. Under the mast, the Roman sailors had placed a coin for luck. ➤

When Pacata's grandmother was young, ships from the Mediterranean brought olives, fish-sauce, wine and other goods to Londinium. This amphora was found in a wrecked ship. There were 6000 olives in it. ▼

The excavation of the Blackfriars ship, showing part of the inside with its curved ribs. On the left you can see an unfinished millstone that had been brought from York. ▼

Suddenly they heard voices crying excitedly, 'A ship! A ship!' Everyone in the forum jostled through the gateway and rushed down the hill to the waterfront. Someone had just landed from the barge that had come from a ship anchored in midstream. It was Valens, Felix' father. He ordered the Council to meet at once in the Basilica, the town hall.

When the Council met, Valens read out the orders he had brought. The Governor was staying up north, and the Procurator was to move his headquarters up there too. Valens had come back to empty the Governor's Palace in Londinium and send all the furniture and state documents up north.

During the next few days, none of the children went to school. Everyone stopped work to watch loaded carts rumbling from the Palace and the Basilica down to the waterfront.

The men who owned barges earned a lot of money ferrying everything from the waterfront to the ships that had arrived to take the goods to the north.

It was a worrying time for the people of Londinium. They couldn't believe that the Governor and Procurator were not coming back. Londinium was the capital of the Province. When Tiro went to the baths, he found his friends complaining that there would be no more work for them. No-one important would live in Londinium now. No new houses would be built, and no-one would be able to afford mosaic floors.

'This is the end of Londinium,' Tiro said. 'It will never be a great city again.' His friends agreed, gloomily.

But Tiro was lucky. One of the last things Valens did before leaving was to pay him. 'You're a good workman, Tiro,' he said. 'There's work for you laying new floors in my parents' house, if you want it. But you'll have to leave Londinium. Their house lies to the south.' Tiro was pleased. At least he'd be able to earn a living, even if he had to leave his friends.

When Pacata heard the news, she knew who had really found the new job for her father. She ran happily off to the statue of the Emperor Hadrian on the bridge. This time she made sure she really was alone!

'It's all right,' she whispered. 'My father's got work! And all because of my shoes!'

She threw something else into the river. It was a little coloured stone she had picked up from her father's workshop.

'Thank you, river god!'

HOW DO WE KNOW?

At the time of the story, the palace at Fishbourne was over 80 years old. The southern half, near the sea, was fenced off and abandoned. Part of the north wing was collapsing and had to be rebuilt. In the alterations, some of the fine features of the old palace were kept, but many new mosaic floors were laid.

Fishbourne Roman Palace, 80 years before the time of the story. Lucius and Mercatilla lived only in the part round the right-hand side of the garden. ➡

This stone carving shows workmen plastering a wall. While the plaster was still wet, it was painted, usually in dark colours. Some panels were painted to look like marble, as it was cheaper to paint a wall than to use real marble. ⬇

⬆ This humpy mosaic floor shows why part of the palace had to be rebuilt. Where the lines are crooked, the floor has sunk.

⬅ A plaster border called *stucco* round the top of the walls in the dining room. The pattern of birds was pressed in with a wooden mould. It was part of the decoration of the old palace.

The Birthday Feast at Fishbourne

Every morning Pacata was woken up by cocks crowing. She was excited to be living in this seaside palace with its big farm. The palace belonged to Felix' grandparents, Lucius and Mercatilla. Valens had kept his promise of finding Tiro work. Tiro was now in charge of laying new mosaic floors in the part of the palace that was being rebuilt. He was using one of the farm buildings as a workshop.

Felix often came to see the new mosaics being laid. If Pacata was there, they would talk. Pacata liked him better than she had done in Londinium. She knew now that his strange gasping was due to an illness. He didn't get these attacks so often now he was living in the country.

Waking up this morning was especially exciting. It was Felix' birthday. After her breakfast of bread and honey, Pacata joined Felix' family in the big room where the household shrine stood. Felix was going to make offerings to his guardian spirit, his 'Genius'. The shrine doors were open. Inside, Pacata could see little statues of the gods and goddesses who protected the family.

Lamps were burning in the shrine, and there was a rich smell of incense. Felix looked very solemn as he carried a silver jug to the shrine. He poured some wine into a shallow dish, a patera. He let a few drops of wine fall on the shrine. Next he carried a plate of food to the shrine.

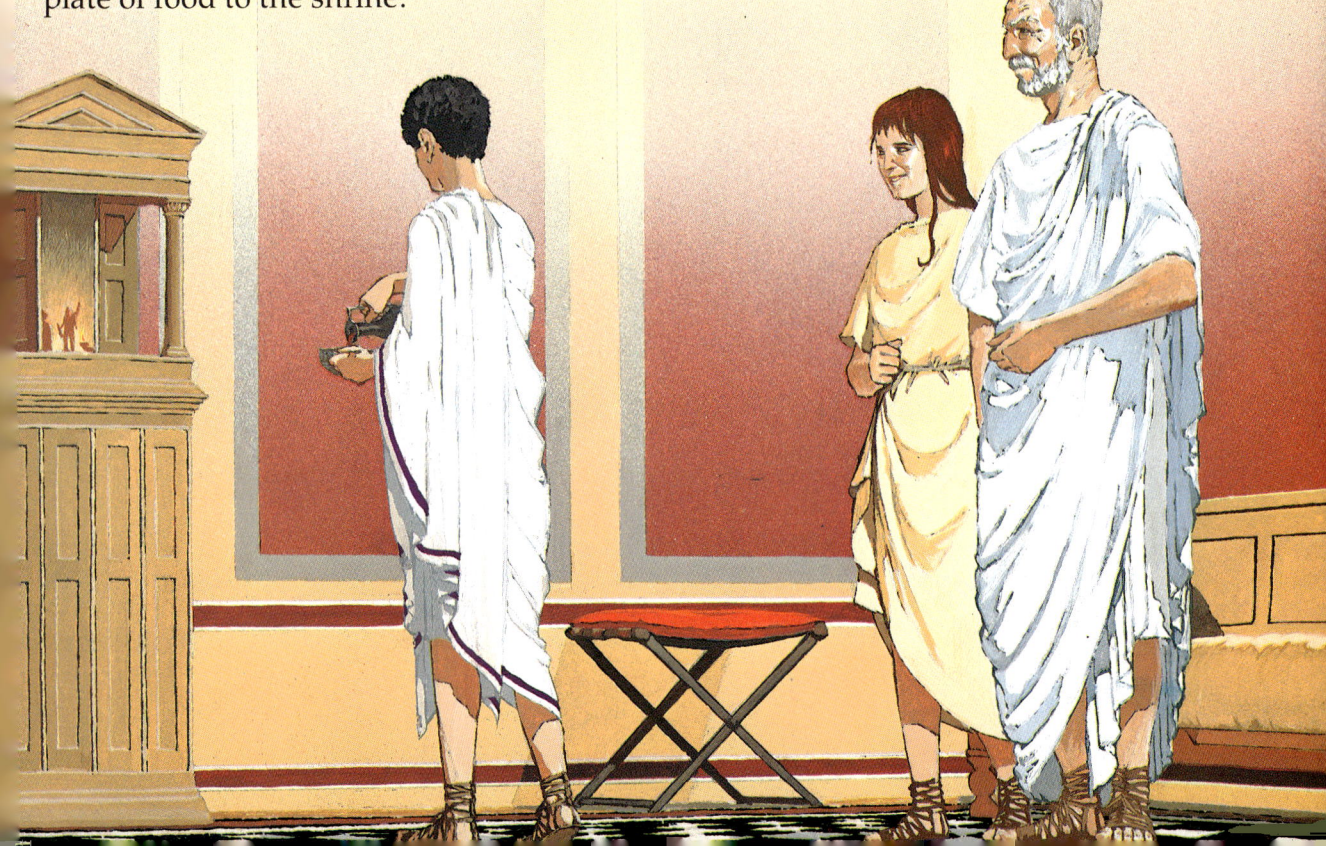

HOW DO WE KNOW?

Roman mosaics were made of small cubes called *tesserae* shaped from stones of different colours: black, white, blue, yellow and brown. Red *tesserae* were made from broken pots. *Tesserae* were laid in fine mortar, which was spread a bit at a time as the mosaicist was setting the *tesserae* in place. Then the spaces between them were filled in, and the mosaic was polished with a smooth stone.

Mosaics could be washed, but slaves had to be careful not to mark the surface when they moved furniture. One mosaic had an inscription in *tesserae* saying, 'Don't hurt the mosaic with a scratchy broom.'

The special foundations laid to keep the mosaic level. First, big bits of stone were set in mortar. This was covered with a layer of coarse mortar. Then the *tesserae* were laid on top. This photograph was taken when a mosaic at Fishbourne had to be lifted for repair. ➔

Tiro's design of a boy riding on a dolphin. ▼

This is the floor from the old palace that Pacata thought it was a pity to spoil by building a wall across it. It has a very clever pattern of boxes that seem to stand up. ▼

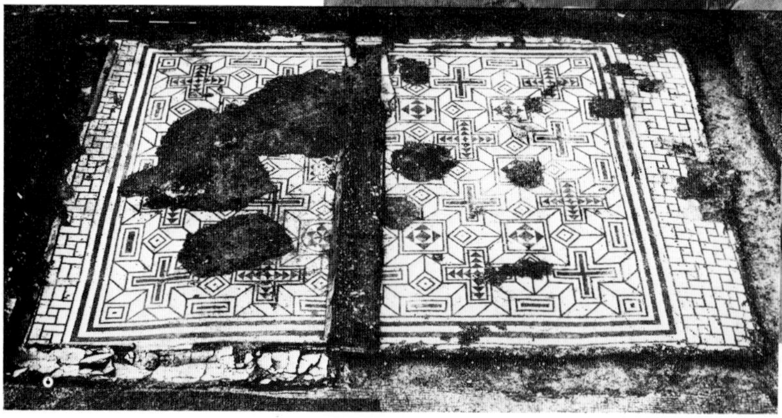

Then his grandfather prayed to the gods and goddesses as he did every day, asking them to look after the family, and to give the farm good crops. The ceremony was over.

'No lessons today!' announced Felix, cheerfully. 'Would you like to come round the farm with me?' asked Lucius. 'We could go for a ride too, if you'd like to try the horse I've bought for boar-hunting.'

'Yes please!' Felix smiled at Pacata and called to her as he hurried after his grandfather, 'See you at my birthday feast tonight!'

'If only the feast could be in the new dining room,' grumbled Mercatilla to Felix' mother. 'I just hope that the new heating system will work. I told Lucius we ought to take up the old mosaic floor and lay the new one over a hypocaust so that the whole floor would get nice and warm. But the builder persuaded us to have the new mosaic laid on top of the old one, with a hot room on each side heated by furnaces under their floors. Mark my words, we'll have the whole house full of smoke from those furnaces.'

Mercatilla hunted through the keys hanging from her belt until she found the key to her storeroom, where the food was kept. Then she bustled off with Felix' mother to tell the cooks what to prepare for the birthday feast. The slaves in the kitchen would be busy all day making special dishes.

Pacata wandered through the part of the palace where the builders were at work. There was a strong smell of wet plaster in the rooms where the walls were being prepared for painting. She saw that one room was being divided into two small ones. Slaves were putting up a wooden partition right across the mosaic floor. Pacata thought it was a pity to spoil this floor. It had a very curious design. Parts of the pattern seemed to stand up like boxes, although they were really flat.

She found her brother Rufus in the new dining room. The new floor looked beautiful. In the middle was a complicated design laid by Tiro himself. It showed a boy riding on a dolphin. Tiro had used lots of tiny little coloured tesserae to make it. Tiro had also laid all the other complicated patterns on the floor himself. The plain background and the border round the edge were being laid by slaves, as this was much easier to do.

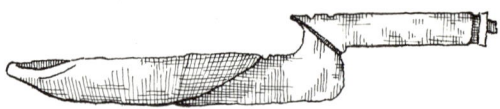

Bronze spoons like this would have been used at Felix' birthday feast. It is worn away more on one side than the other, showing that it was held in the right hand. ➤

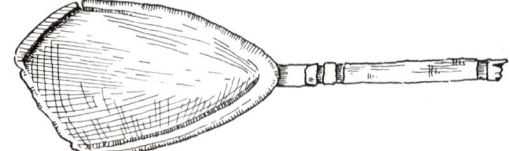

◄ This is the design on a bowl that was found at Fishbourne. It is a beautiful tomato red, and is called 'Samian ware'. The pattern of eagles was made in a mould. Samian ware was used for feasts.

◄ The 'Boy on a Dolphin' mosaic from the new dining room at Fishbourne. The patterns, like the animals and vases, were laid by a master craftsman, but the background and borders were done by less skilled workers, probably slaves. The seahorse at the top is supposed to be the same as the one at the bottom, but it must have been set out by a bad workman, like Rufus.

▲ Pacata's bird from the top border (see arrow on photo).

Rufus was busy laying black tesserae to make a sea-horse.

'It's supposed to be the same as the one Father made over there, isn't it?' asked Pacata. 'The end of the tail's all right, but the middle of the tail is wrong.'

'I don't care if it is!' Rufus exploded. 'I hate this work. One day I'll run away and join the Army. If only I could be in the North keeping the barbarians back behind Hadrian's Wall! Fighting for the Emperor . . . that's a man's life, not this. I don't want to be on my knees all my life, like Father!'

Pacata thought she had better keep out of Rufus' way. She decided to help one of the slaves working on the border. He spread some mortar for her. She knelt down and copied the circle he was making with black tesserae. She filled the centre with white, leaving space for a black leaf. But she found that her leaf was far too small.

'It's not so easy as it looks!' she thought. 'I know, I'll fill up some of the space with a little bird.'

She was concentrating so hard that she did not hear her father come in with Mercatilla. Tiro had come to show Mercatilla the new dining room floor mosaic. She was startled by his angry voice.

'Pacata! Don't spoil the pattern!' Then he shouted to the slave, 'Take that bird out at once!'

But Mercatilla, who was usually so hard to please said, 'No, Tiro, I want it to stay. It will remind me of your daughter Pacata, who makes my serious grandson laugh.'

Pacata was pleased that her bird was going to stay.

HOW DO WE KNOW?

The Romans played many board games with counters made of bone, stone, glass or crystal. A favourite Roman game was *latrunculi* (bandits). The aim was to capture the opponent's *mantra* (sheepfold) and protect your own. Each player had counters that moved differently. *Ordinarii* could only move one square forward or back. *Vagi* could move any number of squares in any direction, and *inciti* could not move at all. Any piece between two enemy ones was captured. The winner was called *Imperator* (Emperor).

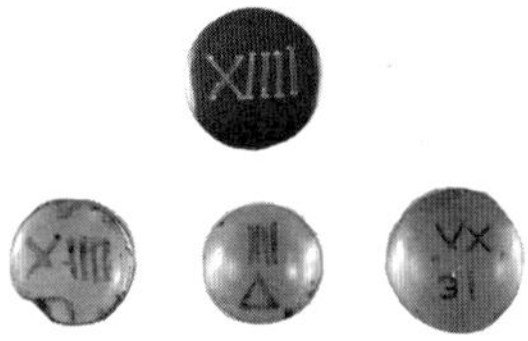

↑ Gaming counters for *latrunculi*.

↑ Stone marked out for a game with counters, complete with dice box, found at Corbridge.

← The Romans did not have books with pages. Writing was in columns on a long scroll, which the reader unrolled with one hand and rolled up again with the other. This boy is reading a scroll to his tutor. They are sitting in basket chairs. Konon gave Felix a scroll like this.

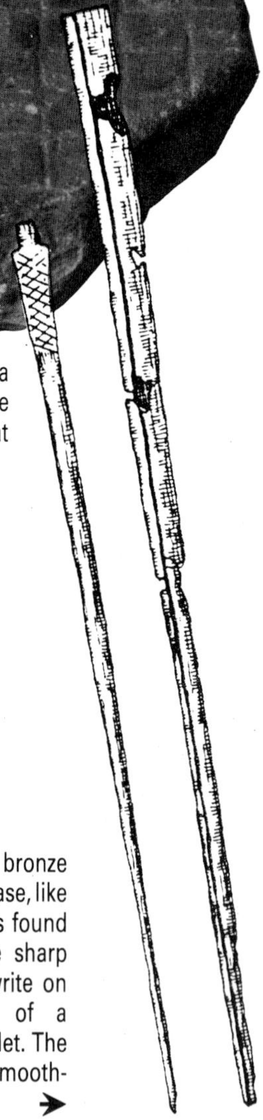

Pacata gave Felix a bronze stylus with its own case, like this one, which was found at Fishbourne. The sharp end was used to write on the wax surface of a wooden writing tablet. The blunt end was for smoothing out mistakes. ➔

That evening, Pacata and Rufus went to Felix' birthday feast. Everyone lay down to eat on couches round a large table. Food and wine were set before them by slaves. Then Lucius poured some wine on to a little altar beside his couch, 'Auguste, patri patriae,' he said. 'Good fortune to the Emperor, the father of our country.'

What a feast it was! The first course was oysters, olives from Italy, dishes of vegetables, and fried snails with wine sauce.

Everyone ate with their fingers, or used a spoon to eat from the big dishes. While they ate, a slave girl played the flute.

For the main course, there was boiled goose with herb sauce, fried fish, and a very special dish called Trojan pig. It was a small pig served whole. When Lucius cut it open, Pacata saw that it was filled with sausages and black puddings. 'Why is it called Trojan pig?' she asked.

'A long time ago,' said Konon, Felix' tutor, 'the Greeks besieged a city called Troy for nine years. They couldn't capture it so they built a huge wooden horse, and hid a lot of soldiers inside it. Then the Greeks pretended to retreat. The Trojans opened the gates and pulled the horse into the city. That night the Greek soldiers crept out of the horse, opened the gates and let the other Greek soldiers into the city of Troy.'

'So the sausages inside are the hidden soldiers!' said Pacata, popping one into her mouth.

The meal ended with fruit and little cakes. Then it was time for the presents. Felix' mother gave him a beautiful silver cup. His grandparents gave him a game called 'bandits' played with counters. Felix was very pleased with this, and said he would teach Rufus how to play it. Konon gave him a scroll, a new book to read. Pacata felt that her present was very small. It was a bronze stylus in a case.

'I need a new sharp stylus,' said Felix, thanking her. 'I'll use it to write to my father to tell him about my birthday.'

Rufus and Pacata said goodnight to Lucius and Mercatilla, and thanked them for the feast. They went out into the garden. The moon shone on the tall cypress trees, and the dew brought out the sweet scent of the briar roses.

Felix caught them up. 'What about a walk round the garden?'

Rufus started to say that he wanted to go to bed, but realised just in time that Felix wanted to walk with Pacata alone. It was strange seeing her walk off with Felix. Until now, she had always done everything with him.

'My little sister's growing up!' he thought.

HOW DO WE KNOW?

The town of Aquae Sulis (Bath) grew up round hot springs. One was sacred to the Celtic goddess Sulis. Engineers built a stone wall on wooden piles round the muddy spring, and lined the basin with lead. The overflow drain is still in use today, nearly 2000 years later. In Victorian times, the spring was covered with concrete. In 1979, this had to be removed. Archaeologists had a chance to dig!

Archaeologists excavating the spring. They found wooden piles, the stone wall, and many offerings thrown into the spring by visitors like Felix, Pacata and Rufus. ➤

▲ 12,000 coins were found. This silver denarius (enlarged) shows the face of Antoninus Pius, who was Emperor at the time of the stories.

◀ Many curses were found. This one lists the names of people who may have carried off a girl named Vilbia. 'Catusminianus' can be read backwards in the second line from the bottom. Writing backwards helped the magic. Curses are useful to archaeologists as they give the names of people who lived in Roman Britain.

The Goddess of the Hot Springs, Aquae Sulis

That summer, Mercatilla was very irritable. Her joints hurt her so much she could hardly walk. Her husband Lucius agreed that she needed treatment, and went to find Tiro.

'We're going to visit friends in Aquae Sulis,' he told him. 'Mercatilla wishes to bathe in the hot waters there, and ask the goddess to heal her. It will be dull for Felix unless he has friends of his own age. Will you let Rufus and Pacata come with us?'

Tiro looked doubtful. 'Rufus has plenty to do here, Sir.'

'The mosaics here are nearly finished,' Lucius went on. 'In Aquae Sulis, Rufus can ask about work for you. I will say you work well.' At last Tiro agreed. He would certainly need another job soon.

Aquae Sulis was a small, busy town with grand houses and many inns. The inns were crowded with sick people who had come from far and wide to pray to the goddess in her great temple, and to bathe in the famous healing waters in the baths nearby.

Next to the baths was a spring, where hot water gushed up from deep in the earth. The spring was surrounded by a wall. A wooden platform was built over part of the spring. On their first morning in Aquae Sulis, Felix, Pacata and Rufus stood together on the platform, looking down into the steamy waters. They each held a silver coin to throw into the spring as an offering to the goddess.

'This is a very holy place!' whispered Felix. Pacata shivered. The water hissed and gurgled as it overflowed into a great drain. They threw in their coins, murmuring a prayer to the goddess. As they looked down, they saw offerings that other people had thrown in: silver cups, gold jewellery, and many coins like theirs.

HOW DO WE KNOW?

People went to the baths every day not only to get clean, but to meet their friends and exchange news. After undressing, they went to a tepid room (*tepidarium*) then to a very hot room (*caldarium*) where they sweated and scraped off the dirt with a strigil. Then they plunged into a cold bath (*frigidarium*) to close their pores. At some baths there was also a very hot, dry room (*laconicum*) like a sauna.

◄ The Great Bath at Bath. It was originally covered with a wooden roof, but this rotted and was replaced with a masonry vault. Part of this fell into the bath and was preserved. You can see it in the photograph above the far end of the bath.

A strigil and an oil flask. In the picture they are about half their real size. ▼

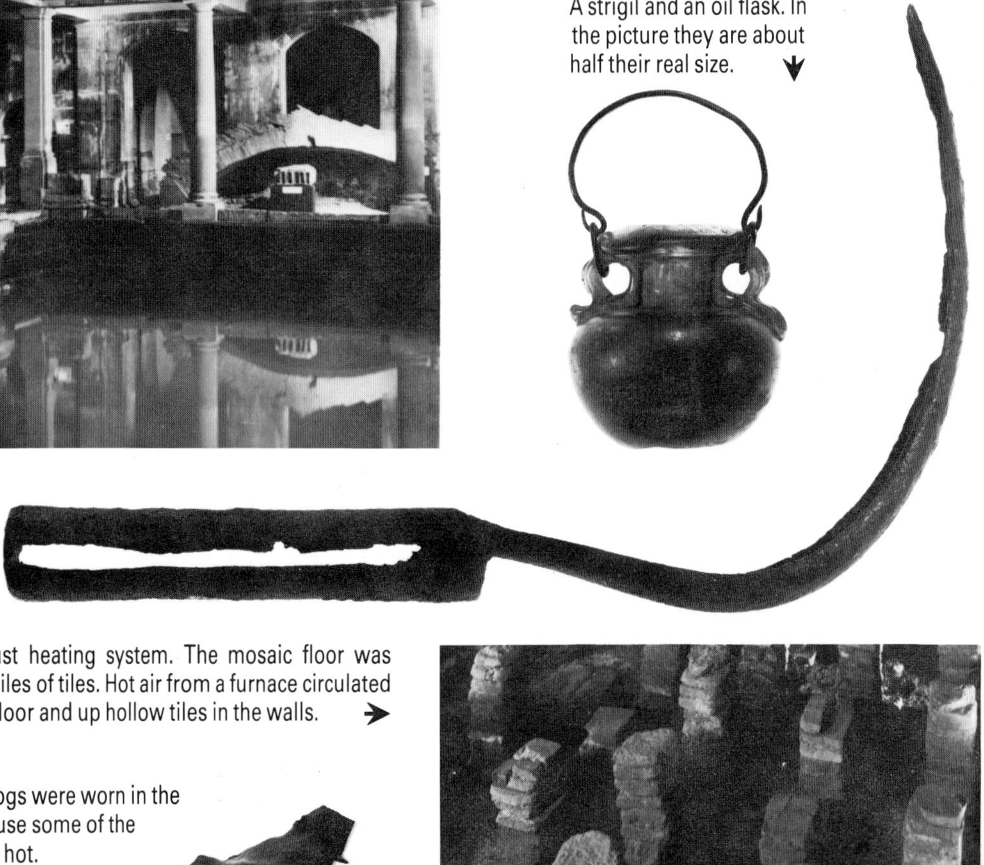

A hypocaust heating system. The mosaic floor was raised on piles of tiles. Hot air from a furnace circulated under the floor and up hollow tiles in the walls. ➤

Wooden clogs were worn in the baths because some of the floors were hot. This one was found at Vindolanda.

As they left the platform, they had to squeeze past a fat man who was boasting that he was going to have his revenge on whoever had stolen his cloak. He waved a sheet of pewter. 'The priest told me what to write on it,' he said. 'When I throw this in, the goddess will read it and kill the thief. Worth all I paid for it!'

Felix' family were waiting for them outside the baths. Mercatilla and Felix' mother were attended by a slave-girl. She was loaded with towels and cases of perfumed oils and cosmetics. Pacata went with them to the entrance to the women's baths.

'Bene lava!' called Felix. 'Enjoy your bath!'

Rufus, Felix and his grandfather and tutor went to the men's baths. They left their clothes in the changing room.

'Come on, Felix,' said Rufus. 'Let's go to the exercise yard.'

Felix was afraid that exercising would make him wheeze. 'Shall I go?' he thought. 'I haven't wheezed for a long time. But if I did, people would stare . . . Rufus,' he said, 'I'd better go with my grandfather.'

He followed his grandfather to a hot pool, where they all relaxed. When they came out, Lucius' slave massaged them with oil. Felix scraped himself with a strigil to get rid of all the dirt and sweat. He plunged into a cold pool and felt really clean.

The longest swimming pool was in a hall with a high wooden roof. Round the walls were seats where men could talk and play dice. The noise there was deafening. Slaves selling wine, cakes and sausages from trays shouted out their wares. Other slaves walked round calling out the time as there were no clocks in the baths. While Felix was swimming, he saw his grandfather buy food and wine. He felt hungry and joined him.

'Have some wine,' Lucius said to him. 'And look up there! I was asking this man why those fellows on ladders are looking at the roof, and he says the wood is rotting with all the steam.'

'A new stone roof would be safer,' Lucius' acquaintance added.

Meanwhile, in the exercise yard, two young men asked Rufus if he would play trigon, a ball game for three people. When they were tired, they went into the baths and talked as they scraped themselves clean. Rufus learned that the men were both soldiers, from a fort on Hadrian's Wall called Vercovicium. They had been sent to Bath to recover from their wounds. Rufus told them he was longing to join the army. They looked at one another. 'We're one short in our group. You could come north with us tomorrow.' There and then, Rufus decided to enlist! No more mosaics for him! Rufus went back to join the others, feeling very happy.

The Romans worshipped Sulis the Celtic goddess of the spring and identified her with Minerva. They built a temple to Sulis-Minerva beside the baths in a walled enclosure. In front of it stood a large altar, on which animals were sacrificed by priests. No services were held in the temple. After sacrificing, people went in for private prayers. They stood to pray, with their hands held out, palm upwards. Then they kissed the feet of the statue of the goddess.

▲ The head of the bronze life-sized statue of Sulis-Minerva that stood inside the temple. Perhaps more of the statue will be found one day.

▲ The front of the temple looked like this. Now only the steps and pieces of decorated stone are left.

Archaeologists excavating the temple steps in 1980. The steps are very worn by the feet of Roman worshippers like Mercatilla and Lucius. ➔

That afternoon, Lucius and Mercatilla took a sheep to the temple as a sacrifice to the goddess. The young people went with them to the big outdoor altar in front of the temple.

Lucius led the sheep to the priest. Assistant priests examined the sheep to make sure it was a perfect animal. Then they killed it, and laid the body on the altar. Another priest, an augurer, cut the sheep open and looked at its liver. He said that the omens were good and the goddess would accept the sheep. Mercatilla smiled. Surely that meant she would be healed.

A piece of meat was cooked in the coal fire that glowed on the altar. The rest of the sheep was carried away for the priests to eat later.

Then Lucius and Mercatilla went up the steps into the gloom of the temple, the home of the goddess. When they came out, Mercatilla told the young people how the golden statue of the goddess had glowed in the light of the temple lamps. She felt better already.

Lucius looked happy. 'We must set up an altar here to thank the goddess. Tomorrow we will find a stonemason and choose the stone. Tonight we'll decide what to have inscribed on it.'

That evening Felix told Pacata that he loved her. He asked her to be betrothed to him. Pacata realised that she loved Felix too.

'But your father will not want you to marry someone like me,' she said sadly. 'You must marry the daughter of an important man.'

'Nonsense!' said Felix. 'I'll write to my father tomorrow.'

Pacata went to ask Rufus what she should do. When she heard he was going away, she pleaded to go with him so that Felix would forget her.

In the morning, Pacata and Rufus had disappeared.

HOW DO WE KNOW?

Housesteads (Vercovicium) was a rectangular fort surrounded by a stone wall with towers. There were four gateways. Roads from these ran to the centre, where the headquarters building with its assembly hall, offices and shrine stood. Nearby were the hospital, granary, and the commander's house. The soldiers lived in ten ten-roomed barracks. Eight men shared a room. The 80 men formed a century under a centurion, who had his own quarters.

← A reconstruction of part of Hadrian's Wall, at Vindolanda.

A stone latrine seat at Ephasus in Turkey. The seats at Housesteads were cut low in front like this. →

A latrine at Housesteads. Along the two long walls were rows of wooden seats, which have not been preserved. Toilet sponges were washed in the gully in the centre, and soldiers washed their hands in the big stone basins. →

↑ The commander's wife would have looked like this lady on a tombstone from Cumbria. She holds a fan. Her son is playing with a pet bird.

Many letters written in ink on thin sheets of wood have been found at Vindolanda. This was sent to the commander's wife by a friend. It says: 'On the third day before the Ides of September, sister, for the day of the celebration of my birthday, I give you a warm invitation to make sure that you come to us...' →

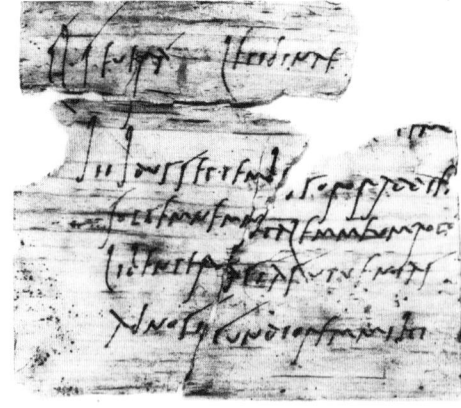

A Day of Surprises at Vercovicium

Summer was turning into autumn. Morning mists dissolved into golden sunshine. Curlews called mournfully over the bare hills. Old soldiers said gloomily that it wouldn't be long before winter came with its rain and hailstorms, when even thick hooded cloaks wouldn't keep the sentries warm.

Rufus and Pacata were now living in the fort of Vercovicium. Pacata was lucky to be living there, as soldiers' families usually had to live in a village some way away from the fort. Only the commander's family lived in the fort, in a large house. But the girl who looked after Pollio, the commander's little son, was ill. The commander's wife, whose name was Vilbia, said that Pacata could live with them and look after Pollio until the girl was better.

Today was a special festival – it was the Emperor's birthday. Pacata dressed Pollio in his best clothes. She was going to take him to the parade in the assembly hall in the middle of the fort.

Rufus was on drains duty, cleaning the camp latrine. It was a dirty job, but he didn't mind. He liked army life much better than laying mosaics. Now he had nearly finished. He scooped out the water from the two stone washbasins, emptying his bucket into the drain with a swish. He had to fetch clean water from the water-tank outside to fill the basins. The men using the latrines along each wall couldn't resist stretching out their legs to try to trip him up. Rufus only grinned.

Rufus was running back to his barracks to get changed for the parade when his centurion stopped him. 'You're on guard at the shrine today, aren't you?' he said. 'Get along to the armourer and say I said you're to have a mail-shirt.'

Rufus felt a real soldier in his shiny mail-shirt. He and his room-mates marched across the hall to the shrine, which opened off it. In front of the shrine were iron grilles. Through the grilles, Rufus saw the sacred standards gleaming in the light of the altar lamps. The big pay-chest full of coins stood there too.

Pacata and Pollio came into the hall and stood near Rufus.

Soon all the soldiers who were not on guard came marching into the hall. Trumpets sounded, and the commander climbed up the steps of the tribunal, a high platform at one end of the hall.

'Today is the birthday of our beloved Emperor,' he said. 'I am going to dedicate an altar and sacrifice an ox. Tonight we will feast.'

Then he read out a letter from the Emperor, telling the soldiers to be brave, and to obey their officers.

HOW DO WE KNOW?

A soldier enlisted for 25 years. He was not allowed to marry, but could keep an unofficial family in the village outside the fort. He could spend his pay in the village inns and shops, but sums were taken from it for his uniform and weapons, food, the camp feasts and burial club. Some was kept as his savings in a chest in the shrine.

Soldiers used to gamble with their pay. This dice was loaded so the owner would keep on winning. It was found at Vindolanda.

Rufus may have carried a shield like this one. It was preserved because it had been charred in a fire, in a fort at Doncaster. The wooden shield was 1.25 metres (4 ft) long, made of oak and alder staves covered with leather, put on wet and glued in place. ▼

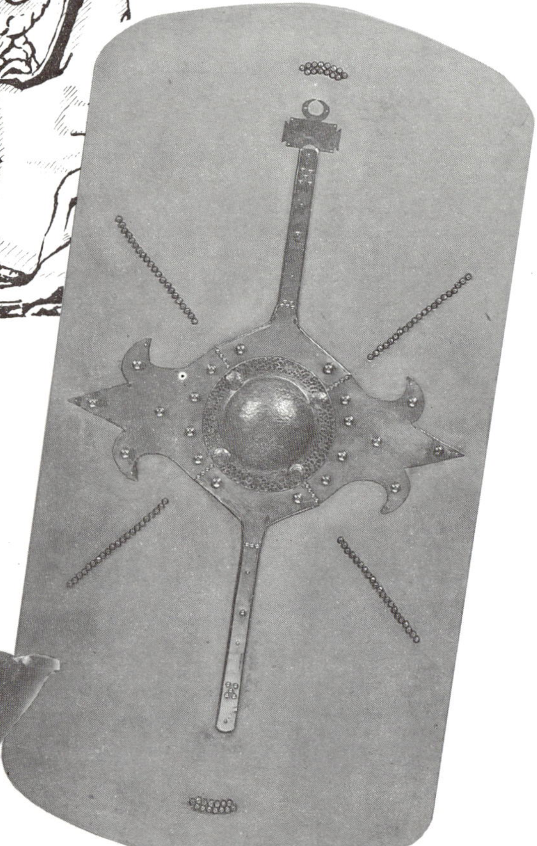

▲ Soldiers carved on a stone column set up by the Emperor Trajan. Rufus would have been dressed like these soldiers in a short tunic and leather trousers. Behind the soldiers are two standards, which were kept in the shrine when the soldiers were not fighting.

Rufus ate out of a bowl like this. This one belonged to someone called Viator. He scratched his name on it. ▼

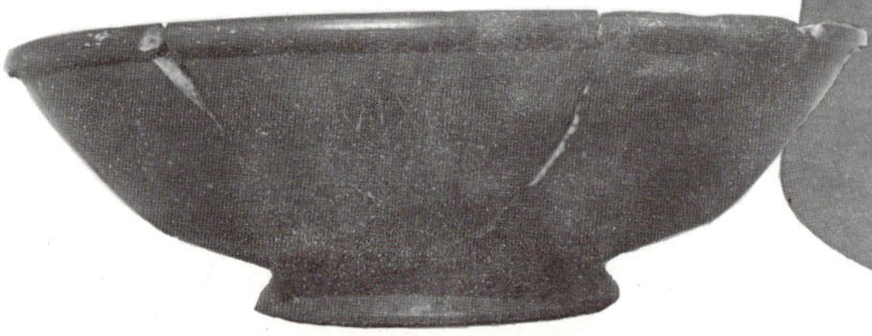

Next, all the soldiers repeated the oath that they had sworn when they had enlisted. Each man raised his right arm and shouted, 'Imperator! Hail, Emperor!'

As the great shout echoed into silence, shrill trumpet calls sounded from outside the hall. The fort was being attacked! Centurions shouted orders, and the troops marched out to battle.

Pacata held Pollio in her arms and ran to Rufus. 'Where can we go?' she cried. Rufus unlocked the shrine door, and pushed them inside. 'Hide behind the altar and don't move!' he ordered. He slammed the door and locked it. Rufus and his friends drew their swords. The sounds of fighting were coming nearer. The barbarians knew where the pay-chest was kept, and a band fought their way into the hall. They saw the shrine and made a rush towards it.

Rufus looked over the rim of his shield as the first barbarian came at him. He pushed the man down with the heavy shield, and slashed him with his sword. He had no time to think before another barbarian was attacking him. He fought desperately, thinking of Pacata and the child inside the shrine, and knowing that he must give his life to save the standards from the enemy. One by one his friends fell wounded. The barbarians pressed forward, their breath hissing through their tangled moustaches.

Suddenly they stopped short, their eyes looking past Rufus in terror. Then they fled out of the hall. Rufus turned round in amazement to see what had scared them. He was startled to see a figure in white holding a standard. It was his sister!

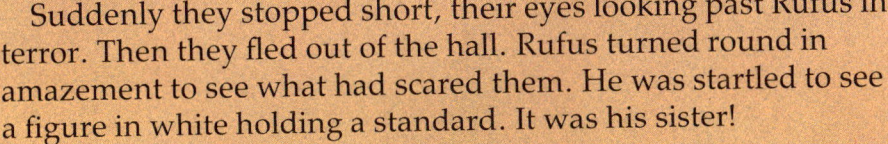

HOW DO WE KNOW?

The hospital at Housesteads was the largest in Britain. The rooms were built round a courtyard, where medicinal herbs may have been grown. There were ten small rooms for patients, an operating theatre, and a latrine and washroom. Roman soldiers had to endure pain bravely. In a doctor's training, he was told to carry on without taking any notice of the noise the patient was making.

Some instruments used by Roman doctors, including: (1) rectal speculum, (2) box possibly used for keeping medicines in, (3) cupping vessel, (4) bronze scoop, spatulae, probes, and a pair of forceps. ➡

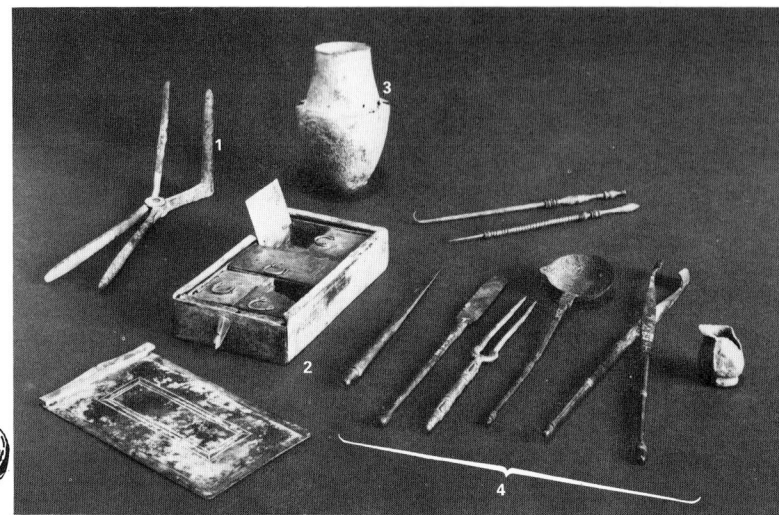

armlets

Soldiers like Rufus who saved a comrade's life in battle were awarded medals of silver and gold, or armlets and torcs (neck-rings), like these.

torcs

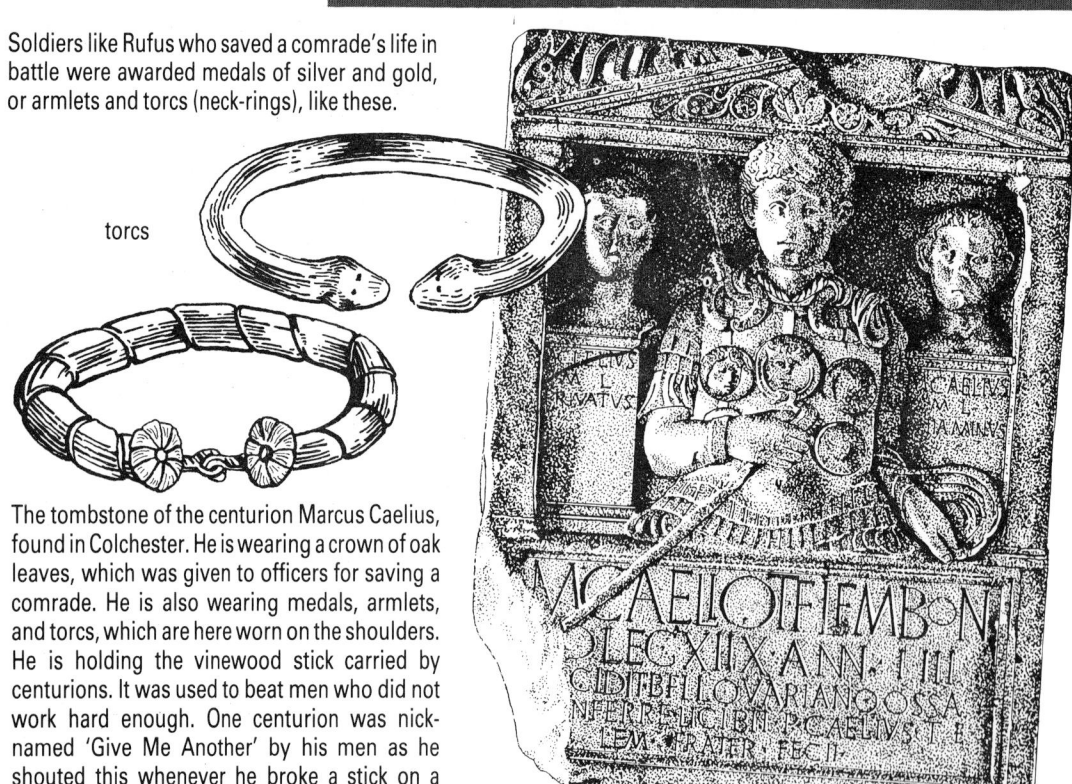

The tombstone of the centurion Marcus Caelius, found in Colchester. He is wearing a crown of oak leaves, which was given to officers for saving a comrade. He is also wearing medals, armlets, and torcs, which are here worn on the shoulders. He is holding the vinewood stick carried by centurions. It was used to beat men who did not work hard enough. One centurion was nicknamed 'Give Me Another' by his men as he shouted this whenever he broke a stick on a man's back. In the end, he was murdered. ➡

'I saw you were the only one left,' Pacata said shakily, 'and I thought I could use the pointed end of this as a spear if they broke down the door. But why did they all run away like that?'

'Perhaps they thought you were a goddess,' said Rufus wearily. 'You even gave me a fright for a moment!'

But another surprise was waiting for the barbarians. A large detachment of cavalry was riding up to the fort, escorting an important visitor. They galloped in through the gate taking the barbarians from the rear. Soon all the barbarians lay dead.

Rufus was carried to the hospital with the other wounded. He had painful sword cuts on his arms and legs, but the mail-shirt had protected the rest of him. The doctor and medical orderlies washed his wounds and bandaged them with herb dressings.

Pacata took Pollio home. There, she had a surprise herself. The important visitor was Valens, and who should be with him but Felix! Valens had come to investigate a customs official who was said to be taking taxes for himself as well as for the Emperor.

'I found out from slaves in the baths at Aquae Sulis that Rufus had met two soldiers from Hadrian's Wall,' said Felix. 'So I guessed where you had gone. I rode up to Eboracum to see my father. You know I wanted to ask him something.'

Pacata's heart was beating very fast and she couldn't speak.

'Felix has told me that he wants to marry you', said Valens, looking kindly at Pacata. 'I have known your family for many years. If your father is willing, I agree to your betrothal.'

Pacata couldn't believe her ears but it was true! The first person to hear the news was Rufus. Pacata and Felix went to see how he was, but they had to wait because the commander was visiting the hospital to talk to the wounded men.

Rufus' centurion told the commander that Rufus had saved the lives of his room-mates by fighting on even after he had been badly wounded. 'He saved the standards and pay-chest from falling into enemy hands, too, Sir,' he ended.

'As well as my son's life, I hear,' said the commander, his grim face relaxing into a smile. 'You've made a good start, Rufus. Carry on like this, and you'll be an officer one day.'

When Pacata and Felix came in, Rufus had a surprise for them as well. 'I'm going to be awarded the torcs and armlets,' he said faintly, 'and then I'm going to go on leave to get well.'

'How proud father and mother will be!' said Pacata. 'They can't be cross now about you being a soldier instead of laying mosaics.'

'And we'll all travel south together,' said Felix firmly. 'No more running away!'

What happened next . . .

Now that Felix was 14, he was grown-up. There was another big feast at Fishbourne, where Valens saw his son put on the robe worn by men. Felix and Pacata were betrothed. Felix gave Pacata a jet pendant with their faces carved on one side, and clasped hands on the other. Pacata stayed at Fishbourne to learn how to look after a big house with many slaves. Felix went to Gaul (France) to study law and public speaking. When he came back, he was appointed to the Procurator's staff. He and Pacata were married. Tiro and his wife stayed in the west of Britannia, where people were building many new houses. He had a lot of work and became a rich man. Rufus enjoyed life in the army, and became a centurion. He always remembered his first fight at the shrine at Vercovicium.

Where you can see the things in this book and other things like them:

LONDON	Museum of London
	The British Museum
FISHBOURNE	Fishbourne Roman Palace and Museum, Chichester
BATH	Roman Baths Museum
HADRIAN'S WALL	Housesteads Roman Fort Museum
	Vindolanda Roman Fort and Museum
	Museum of Antiquities, Newcastle-upon-Tyne
Cardiff	National Museum of Wales
Chester	Grosvenor Museum
Cirencester	Corinium Museum
Colchester	Colchester and Essex Museum
County Durham	Bowes Museum
Dover	Roman Dover Tourist Centre
Edinburgh	Royal Museum of Scotland (Queen Street)
Leicester	Jewry Wall Museum and Site
Lincoln	City and County Museum
Reading	Museum and Art Gallery
St Albans	Verulamium Museum
York	Yorkshire Museum